Churnet
Guide & Souvenir

Lindsey Porter

MORREDGE TO CHEDDLETON

The Churnet rises in a number of streams flowing westwards from Merryton Low (1,603ft OD), the third highest point in Staffordshire. These wild moors of Morredge are very accessible to the motorist who drives along the fine road which extends from the Royal Cottage Inn on the A53 Buxton to Leek road. For some miles this road is the border of the Peak District National Park, with extensive views on either side.

Tittesworth Reservoir Visitor Centre

Meerbrook, Leek, Staffs ST13 8SW
Modern purpose-built centre, two circular trails plus conservation area and bird hides; fishing; restaurant, gift shop. Entry free. Tel: 01538 300400. www.stwater.co.uk

Two miles below Upper Hulme the river, having received small tributaries from the Roaches, enters Tittesworth Reservoir. The first dam was constructed as early as 1858, and has been raised twice since.

At Leek the Churnet, as one might expect, has provided water for industry for a considerable period. It provides a very soft water for dyeing and Leek became well known for its dyes, including the famous 'Raven Black'. In fact it was here that Sir Thomas Wardle developed new dyes from vegetable sources in Victorian times. It was a revolutionary discovery in its day. Beautiful examples of embroidery using these new dyes may still be seen. Perhaps the finest locally surviving example is the alter frontal in St Edward's Church. It is not used on a daily baasis and is usually kept in a glass case.

Victorian Altar Frontal, St Edward's Church, Leek

In the flat meadows adjacent to the river at Abbey Green just upstream from the cottages and the first Leek dyeworks on the river, lie the remains of Dieulacress Abbey, which was founded in 1214. The abbey was of the Cistercian Order and had been previously established at Poulton near to Chester. Little remains of the abbey following the dissolution in 1538. A few piers and foundation stones survive together with various carvings built into the buildings of the Abbey Farm, close to the Abbey Inn. Unfortunately the remains are on private ground and not open to the public.

The town of Leek is bounded on two sides by the river, being originally founded on a piece of high ground above it. From early times, the town has been a market centre, and it was given a Royal Charter to hold a

Sugden architecture at the Natwest Bank, Derby Street, Leek

weekly market and annual fair in 1296 by King John. Although the weekly cattle market is still a vital part of the town's life, it was moved in 1960 to the outskirts of the town. Previously the cattle market existed on the site of the bus station and Smithfield shopping centre.

The textile and the associated dyeing industry using the soft waters of the Churnet used to be the main employers, but it has been eclipsed by overseas manufacturers. Many former mills now are apartments or used by the pine and antiques market. To the visitor, however, perhaps the main streets offer the most interest. A considerable number of the Victorian buildings were designed by the local firm of Sugdens, whose qualities stand out today in the many Arts and Crafts properties that survive.

The town boasts of a very fine and ancient church, parts of which date back to before the Conquest. There are equally ancient crosses and the church is well worth a visit. Look out for its beautiful circular or rose windows and the grave stone near the tower's west door that alleges that its occupier died aged over 400 years old! Bonny Prince Charlie passed through here on his way to Derby in December 1745, and again a few days later on his way north, sleeping one night at the Vicarage and the other at the adjacent stone-built house at the top of the Market Place. The latter building was the birthplace of Thomas Parker, who distinguished himself as a Lord Chancellor and became the first Earl of Macclesfield, only to be impeached for £30,000! Leek is a fascinating place if one cares to take an interest, but our story is with the river and it is to that subject that we must return.

The town had a corn mill on the river, at Mill Street (the main road to Macclesfield west of the old Parish Church), which fortunately has survived. Thanks to a preservation trust and the generosity of Leek people, the mill has been restored. The Leek Corn Mill is attributed to James Brindley who had a workshop close to the mill, possibly at 189-193 Mill Street, that had the appearance of a former workshop and large gates to allow access for a horse and cart. Unfortunately the latter property has now been demolished.

Left: Greystones, Stockwell Street, Leek

Below: St Edward's Parish Church, Leek

Brindley Mill

Mill Street, Leek, Staffs ST13 6BL
Waterwheel driven corn mill, dated 1752.
Associations with James Brindley. See corn being ground!
Tel: 01538 381446. www.brindleymill.net

The mill itself is open to visitors and although a portion of the mill was demolished for road widening purposes in 1948 all the machinery is intact. On the ground floor is situated the usual pitwheel, wallower and other gears with three pairs of millstones above. The roof structure is particularly interesting – the tie beam being curved upwards in the middle to give sufficient head room. It consists of two pieces of timber that match exactly, for they were cut from the same crooked tree. The wooden water wheel is undershot and 16ft in diameter, turning at fifteen revolutions a minute.

The Brindley 'hallmark' is found in the doorway and windows that have arches and keystones similar to those on Brindley's canals. Inside the mill there is also a stone bearing the initials T. I. (J.) and J. B., together with the date 1752 when the mill was probably built.

Rudyard Lake Steam Railway

Rudyard Station, Rudyard, Leek, Staffs ST13 8PF
3 mile return trip alongside Rudyard Lake on narrow gauge steam train.
Tel: 01995 672280.   www.rlsr.org

From the mill, the river flows away from the town and skirts around Westwood to the border of the town again on the south-east side. It passes within 1½ miles of Rudyard Lake, a local beauty spot popular with yachtsmen. The lake is really a reservoir, built in 1793 and ingeniously using a feeder from the River Dane to maintain the water level in both the Caldon and the Trent and Mersey Canals. Rudyard Kipling was named after the village, where his parents apparently spent their honeymoon about the year 1860. The canal feeder and river both run down a deep valley. The feeder runs until it reaches the Leek branch of the Caldon Canal, that passed over the river on an aqueduct. Although the latter remains, the arm of the canal from here to Leek has been obliterated by industrial development. From here, one can walk along the Leek arm, except for a short stretch of canal which is tunnelled, to Wall Grange. Here, where the canal is crossed by a road

Rudyard Lake

Above: Market day at Leek. Below: The Holly Bush Inn, Denford, nr Longsdon

bridge, one can leave the Leek branch and join the main canal by walking down the road, over a brook and the railway line to reach the canal. Alternatively, one can continue an extra mile or so to where the two branches join at Denford locks, which are worth a visit. The locks were built in 1842 and have side ponds to conserve water. The canal can be crossed by a fine iron towpath bridge at this point.

At Denford the main canal locks down and passes under the Leek arm which is carried by a large stone and brick aqueduct at Hazelhurst, near a canal keeper's cottage. The canal soon turns to front Hazelhurst cottages and a canal public house – the 'Holly Bush'. Returning to Wall Grange one can trace the remains of the old brick works that overlook the canal on the south bank and a huge quarry face at the rear where the raw materials were quarried. From its source to Wall Grange there has been no continuous road or path near the river, but from here the walker can follow the towpath of the Caldon Canal to Cheddleton, and onwards to some of the best scenery in the Churnet Valley.

Above: Hazelhurst Aqueduct. Below: Cast iron bridge at Denford Locks

CHEDDLETON TO FROGHALL

Although industrial enterprises exist at Cheddleton and Froghall, it is difficult to believe that the rural area of Consall Forge (and Oakamoor below Froghall) were once the centres of great industry. The river soon flows through a wooded countryside as lovely as any in the county. Similarly the vast enterprise of Bolton's Copper Works at Froghall is soon forgotten in the leafy miles towards Oakamoor, which up to a few decades ago also produced copper.

Cheddleton Flint Mill

Leek Road, Cheddleton, Leek, Staffs ST13 7HL
Canal side flint mill with two working waterwheel-driven mills. Entry free
Tel: 01782 502907
www.ex.ac.uk/-akoutram/cheddleton-mill

At Cheddleton, an old village which still has its stocks intact under the churchyard wall, opposite the Black Lion Inn, the canal passes an old flint mill that has been preserved. The age of the mill or mills, for there are two waterwheels each serving its own mill, is obscure, but it has been traced back to 1694. The works were purchased by a preservation trust in 1969 and have been restored. Many examples of old grinding machinery from other potters' millers have been brought to the museum. The mill machinery is still in working order and can be seen in operation every Saturday and Sunday. In addition, Mintons, the china manufacturers, have donated a Robey steam engine complete with fly wheel which is also in working order, although its motive power for demonstration purposes is now electricity and not steam.

The Caldon Canal passes the works and was used to bring flint to be calcined in two brick-lined kilns that were built on the canal bank. All the items of machinery are accompanied by descriptions and a guide is available giving the known history of the mill and of how the mill machinery operates. One of the two mills has previously been a corn mill and there is some evidence to suggest that one of the mills was intermittently used for grinding flint, corn and colour (iron and other oxides to serve as pigments in paints and glazes).

A preserved narrowboat, the *Vienna*, a Fellows, Moreton and Clayton boat, is permanently moored by the flint mill.

The canal then runs at the side of a former paper works and is soon joined by the railway. This appears from a tunnel at Leekbrook junction, where the main line, now removed, and which ran through Leek to Macclesfield, is met by branch lines to the Potteries and Cauldon Lowe Quarry.

The 'Vienna' at Cheddleton Flint Mill

Churnet Valley Railway

Cheddleton Station, Station Road, Cheddleton, Leek ST13 7EE
Steam or diesel services through the Churnet Valley to Froghall Station, stops at Consall Station. Tea rooms either end.
Tel: 01538 360522
www.churnet-valley-railway.co.uk

Shortly after leaving Cheddleton Mill the valley is crossed by a minor road at Basford Bridge where there is a canal side pub, 'The Boat'. It is adjacent to the preserved Cheddleton Station, where on certain days you can get a steam or diesel service to Consall and Froghall Stations. It makes a useful way of combining a towpath walk one way and a leisurely train journey in reverse. Below Basford Bridge there is no public road running down the valley until Oakamoor is reached, and the rambler can enjoy the delights of a truly beautiful valley. After approximately a mile and a half, at Oakmeadow Lock, the river is canalised as far as Consall Forge.

A little way above Oakmeadow Lock the Churnet is joined by the Coombes Brook, which in its upper section is a nature reserve. Only two paths cross this part of the Coombes Valley – the 'Surprise View' path from Ferny Hill to Sharpcliffe, and the Butter Cross path from Cheddleton to Whitehough.

RSPB Coombes Valley

Six Oaks Farm, Bradnop, Leek, Staffs ST13 7EU
Nature reserve with 1½ miles of nature trails. Entry free
Tel: 01538 384017
www.rspb.org.uk

Above the lower part of the Coombes Valley lies Basford Hall, still privately occupied and still owned by a Sneyd descendant, whose family used to possess a substantial part of this area, and planted many of the woodlands. The Sneyds also owned nearby Ashcombe, Woodland and Belmont Halls at one time.

Right & below: Consall Nature Centre and Reserve. See p.16 for details

Consall Forge at the Black Lion Inn

Consall Forge lies about half a mile below Oakmeadow Lock and is extremely picturesque. A road exists to Consall Forge from Consall village, but there is only public car parking for visitors to the Black Lion Inn. The road is unmade below the Nature Centre, which can give details of walks and nature trails in the area. There is car parking here.

As well as the obvious footpath route along the canal, there are other paths giving access to Consall Forge. The name is derived from the seventeenth-century iron forge that existed here. There is a lot to interest the visitor at Consall Forge, and also in the valley from here down to Froghall, whether one's interest is in flora and fauna, passing boats, or industrial history. The area has not escaped industrial use, but has recovered from this much better than most industrialised valleys. Now one has to search the leafy glades in order to find the remains of old mills, tramways, ironstone mines and quarries which

the Victorians would have seen, and in summer nature proves very successful in hiding the scars that industry produced.

Consall Forge is now a sleepy hamlet with a few cottages and a public house – The Black Lion – that affords a pleasant stop in which to appreciate the tranquillity of the area. It is very popular, especially on sunny weekends. Here the canal and river part company. The river falls over a weir at the site of the old forge. On the west bank of the valley a cottage standing high up is known as Halfway House – apparently regarded by boatmen as being halfway between the two extremes of the old canal at Etruria and Uttoxeter. Consall Forge was also apparently 34 miles and 34 locks from Preston Brook, the northerly end of the Trent and Mersey canal.

Retracing one's steps upstream a little, a battery of large lime kilns can be seen. From here one can trace an old horse-drawn tramway that gradually climbs uphill from the kilns as one walks upstream.

Consall Station

Consall Nature Park

Visitor Centre and nature trails in the Churnet Valley.
Access via Consall village.
Entry free
Tel: 01782 550939

After about three hundred yards the old tramway crossed over a cutting which gives access to an old quarry. Here stone for the canal was cut and dressed for the necessary masonry, and no doubt for local building needs as well. The tramway climbed out of the valley, passed the rear of Consall Old Hall and wound its way across the fields towards the Potteries. Presumably the line lasted until the North Staffordshire Railway arrived in the 1840s.

Opposite the Black Lion Inn the canal crosses under the railway after leaving the river, and the two run side by side for some distance. Here the railway encroached upon the canal, which was filled in down one side. Above the retaining wall the canal-side railway platform was cantilevered out over the canal. Removed decades ago, it has been replaced (Easter, 2005). The wooden station buildings have been rebuilt and the station serves the preserved railway. A terraced row of old railway cottages serves as a reminder of the area's former importance.

Walking down the towpath, just below the station, the ruins of Crowgutter Mill are reached. Messrs Podmores ground flint here until

1947 but damage to the water pipes in the severe winter of that year was so bad that the mill was abandoned. Vandalism took its toll and little is now left of the buildings. Just below Crowgutter the valley is crossed by London Bridge, named after a London-based mining company which worked coal and iron ore close-by in the nineteenth century. The river bridge is relatively new, however, and was built by the Podmores to gain access to their mill after the previous structure had been swept away. The road to Consall was formerly a tramway from an old mine that brought ore and coal down to the canal and railway in the valley.

Half a mile or so below London Bridge one reaches the last, but now closed, flint mill in the valley. Initially it was built with one waterwheel but a further two were added in the large brick-built building. These two huge wheels, sadly now scrapped, were known as *Jack* and *Jill*. The power and hence the vibration which they produced is evident in the large number of tie bars that support the building. The canal is quite wide at the top of the lock adjacent to the old mill, for this was a further point where iron ore was loaded. The mines on the south side of the valley were served by a tramway which crossed the river and the railway, on a tall spindly wooden bridge. With luck it is still possible to pick up small pieces of red iron-ore from around the point where the bridge commenced, close to the footpath to Kingsley.

Froghall Wharf Canal Boat Trips

Froghall Wharf, Foxt Road, Froghall, Stoke-on-Trent ST10 2HJ
2 1/2 hour public trips twice a week.
Tel: 01538 266486

Christmas on the Caldon, nr Cherry Eye Bridge

Below the mill, the towpath passes through a leafy glade until a metal cross-over bridge is reached. A quick look at the bridge reveals the railway influence after the canal was purchased by the railway. Just before the bridge is a petrifying stream by the towpath. This unusual feature has been known for a long time and was noted by Dr Plot in 1686 in his *Natural History of Staffordshire* – although the canal did not exist then of course. Across the railway line there stood until recently a row of cottages, now demolished. There was no access to these other than along the canal towpath and they obtained their water from the petrifying well.

From the metal bridge it is a short walk to the Cherry Eye Bridge that takes its name from the old Cherry Eye Mine where iron ore was worked until 1921. The mine is situated high in the wood on private land. The area around the bridge is particularly pretty and the setting well worth a walk from Froghall, a distance of about a mile or so. On the Froghall side of the bridge, where the railway crosses the river, is the site of the wharf where ore from Cherry Eye Mine was loaded into boats.

FROGHALL TO ALTON

At Froghall the large copper works has spread across the valley, but it is still possible to see from the towpath Alfred S. Bolton's initial buildings, erected in 1890 as an extension to the former Oakamoor mills. The canal crosses under the Ipstones Road in a tunnel 75 yds long just before Froghall Wharf. It is difficult at first glance to appreciate the buildings and industrial activity which formerly existed here. Nature has reclaimed much of her own and the County Council have lent a hand, levelling, seeding and planting daffodils for the spring time. A picnic site has been established here and Froghall makes an excellent base for exploring the Churnet and Caldon Canal. Some buildings remain, including a large battery of lime kilns, and it is worth looking a little closer, whether your interest is industrial history, botany or whatever.

If you have parked the car at this point, walk between the buildings on the west side of the road to Foxt, to where you can cross a bridge over an old lock recently refurbished (2005). This was the first lock on the Uttoxeter branch, which was opened in 1811 and served the lower part of the valley until 1849, when it was closed and the majority of the canal bed used for the line of the new Churnet Valley Railway. Immediately below the lock can be seen the turning area of the canal, where stone-laden boats began their journey from Froghall. It is now a new berth for boats at the limit of the canal.

Returning to the road, the buildings here were old railway company buildings, but the remaining one opposite was obviously a canal-side warehouse.

Returning to the roadway, one can now walk along the last few yards of canal on the east side of the road. The former activity of men breaking stone and loading boats has been replaced by fishermen and pleasure boats. At the far end of the site stand a few cottages and the start of the tramway to Cauldon Quarries, or Froghall Quarries as they were more correctly known. There were four lines in all, a temporary one of 1777, replaced in 1780 by a more substantial line that served until 1804 when John Rennie was commissioned to rebuild the line. In 1849 however, a more direct route was built which survived until 1920, when the stone was taken out on the Waterhouses branch line, and the tramway was closed.

The lime kilns are worth examining, and a good view of the area is gained by walking up the track to the top of them. Examination of the right hand end (by the Foxt road) shows that practically every stone has its own mason's mark.

A recent development has been the rebuilding of Froghall Station in traditional style. There is a tea room here and trains run back to Cheddleton. Refreshments are also available at the Railway Inn and at Froghall Wharf.

It is worth mentioning that one can return along the edge of the valley, on the Kingsley side, towards Consall Forge, on foot or by

Left: Rebuilt Froghall Station
Below: Oakamoor

Hawksmoor Nature Reserve

On B5417
Cheadle-Oakamoor road
National Trust 300 acre reserve opened in 1927.
Various trails, open all year round.
Tel: 01538 703685

car. The lane is not very wide but well worth visiting for the fine views down into the valley and across to Ipstones Edge. Below Froghall, the rambler is denied access except for a limited number of paths. This is a great pity, made worse by the loss of a footbridge over the Churnet some years ago, which has never been replaced. Fortunately, between Kingsley Holt and Greendale a path does exist that drops down to the river and allows some exploration of the area.

South of the river and just above Oakamoor is the Hawksmoor Nature Reserve which well repays further exploration. Within its 250 acres, around fifty species of birds have been recorded; also foxes, badgers, hares, weasels, grey squirrels and grass snakes.

It is of interest that a Hawksmoor swallow ringed by J. R. B. Masefield in May 1911, was caught 7,000 miles away in Natal in late 1912! This long legacy of interest in wildlife is still alive today, and both the keen naturalist and the novice find a visit to Hawksmoor rewarding. There are three nature trails; a $2^1/_2$ mile long trail starts at the main gates, and two other trails ($1^1/_2$ miles) start at East Wall Farm, the site of medieval iron furnaces. A booklet describing the trails is available.

Oakamoor now presents the appearance of a sleepy village but a quick look around reveals evidence of previous activity. In addition to the considerable number of old properties, there is also the delightful millpond that falls over a weir by the road bridge. Below the bridge, the large grassy platform used as a picnic area marks the site of Thomas Bolton's copper works. This was an old iron rolling mill which was later converted into a tinplate mill. In 1790 it was purchased by Thomas Patten and Co, who developed the site considerably as a copper-rolling mill. Patten also had brass and copper works at Cheadle together with a wire and strip mill at Alton (further downstream). In 1828, the whole concern was concentrated at Oakamoor and considerably expanded. Bolton's purchased the works in 1852 and were responsible for drawing the wire for the first successful Atlantic cable in 1856, mostly at this works.

The works was run by Thomas Bolton's son Alfred Sohier Bolton and his brother Francis (the father having died in 1854). A. S. Bolton was a very astute man who recognised the importance of the growing telegraphy industry. As a result the works expanded considerably until the site became too cramped for further development and an extension was built at Froghall. The piecemeal development of the Oakamoor works together with its great age led to its closure, and in 1963 the firm's activities were transferred to Froghall.

The site has now been levelled and seeded to make a picnic area. A stop here should be combined with the walk up Cotton Dell nearby. It is a delightful path amid leafy glades and should not be missed. From Oakamoor to Alton a choice of route is possible, and a round trip is well worth while. If one takes the road via Farley (signposted to Alton Towers), one first passes Moor Court, the former home of A. S. Bolton which he built in 1861 together with its two lodges. The real point of interest is Farley village, and although there has been some recent selective development, the majority of the properties are old and interesting. They are however, surpassed by the beauty of Farley Hall, formerly owned by the Earls of Shrewsbury and occupied by the Bill family for a considerable time. Charles Bill's initials appear on a gable wall. During World War II, the hall was used as a Youth Hostel but it is now a private residence again and is not open to the public.

Opposite page: Oakamoor Bridge. Above: The Rambler's Retreat

    The alternative road is narrow and follows the river valley to Alton. Oakamoor station was just off this road, but all the buildings have been demolished. Although the road is narrow, its leafy glades, with glimpses towards the Propect Tower at Alton Towers make it worthwhile. Close to Alton, at a bend in the road, is an open space with a footpath sign to Dimmingsdale. It is worth parking the car here, to explore Dimmingsdale. The unusually-designed house here is now the Rambler's Retreat, a popular restaurant and tea room serving visitors arriving by car, cycle or on foot. Shortly beyond this, one arrives at an old corn mill, now a private house, but still with the millgear intact. Above the buildings are the mill ponds, that are well worth looking at. The mill is marked on the OS maps as a Smelting Mill and indeed in the eighteenth century it was a lead smelting mill. The short return walk should be continued over the Alton-Oakamoor road to Lord's Bridge which spans the former railway. As well as being an old driveway to Alton Towers it was a popular point for railway photographers to record the steam trains rounding the bend above the bridge on the down line. Here also, one can see the old canal that is clearly visible and marked on most maps.

ALTON TOWERS

No trip to the Churnet Valley is complete without at least one visit to Alton Towers. The Towers are the former home of the Earls of Shrewsbury and today is famous for its rides (dispensing thrills galore and sheer terror depending upon your constitution) and much more in its huge pleasure park. The house was built to impress – regardless of cost or contemporary thoughts on architecture or garden layout. Today the huge house is in ruins but its impressiveness is still its hallmark and the gardens even more so. Let us however, start at the beginning; this is particularly important as it enables us to appreciate the work that Charles Talbot started.

The beginnings were in the early nineteenth century. Charles Talbot was the fifteenth Earl of Shrewsbury, the premier Earl of England, whose seat was at Heythorp in Oxfordshire. He was an extremely wealthy man and owned several large estates including one at Alton, where there was a house known as Alverton Lodge (Alverton being the old name for Alton). The Lodge was occupied by the earl's bailiff, who was responsible for the affairs of the estate. The initial idea was

Alton Towers

Alton, Stoke-on-Trent, Staffs
Internationally renowned theme park.
Tel: 0870 458500
www.altontowers.com

to landscape the grounds, and work began in 1812. The grounds stood on sandstone which was easy to drain and produced richer soil than the shallow soil of the adjacent limestone hills. In 1814 the earl moved to the Lodge in order to supervise the work.

In the same year an Enclosure Act was passed enabling much of the surrounding countryside to be incorporated into the scheme. Up to his death in 1827, the grounds were gradually laid out and the house enlarged in the Gothic style. It was renamed Alton Abbey and from a contemporary print it is easy to see which parts date from this period. Charles was succeeded by his nephew John, who continued the work, and when the house at Heythorp was destroyed by fire in 1831, Alton became the permanent seat of the earl. Further extensions took place and the name changed again to Alton Towers.

Charles can be regarded as responsible for the creation of the grounds and the majority of the north front of the mansion (ie, the part facing the lake).

On the other hand, John appears to have concentrated on bringing the mansion up to a standard which befitted the splendour of the grounds. Several architects were employed including Abraham and Fradgley (a local man). In 1832 the earl met A. W. Pugin and a friendship developed between the two men. Pugin was employed at Alton thereafter, and the entrance lodge, the decoration of the chapel (erected previously), the banqueting hall and conservatory were designed by him. In addition he designed the 'Castle' on the other side of the river Churnet that looks as though it has been plucked from the Rhineland.

The house itself was enormous and was said to have been built without domestic consideration. Today most of the walls support a roof top walk, all the floors have been removed and it is difficult to appreciate how majestic the house really was. The entrance was on the east side – nearest the gardens. Either side of the entrance are statues of Talbot dogs. The actual entrance hall is huge in height but relatively small in plan, given scale by the truly massive wooden doors. This brought one into the armoury. Some idea of its former condition can be gauged by the stained glass windows that are still intact. Beyond this, the rest of the house is in ruin and not open to the public.

The armoury formerly led into the picture gallery which housed the valuable collection of paintings purchased from Bonaparte's mother. Beyond this was the Octagon where one could turn right into Pugin's conservatory and so into the main body of the house, which housed the state rooms and the private chapel.

These buildings surround the private garden of the Countess and this is still known as 'her Ladyship's garden'. One room is easy to locate. Today it is a gaunt shell of immense size, fortunately still with its slate roof. This is the principal dining room or banqueting hall. The majority of its stained glass window remains and can be seen from the front that faces the lake.

A walk around the exterior of this immense house leaves one with a feeling of sorrow that the place has been reduced to ruins. Yet even so, Charles Talbot's intentions, pursued further by his nephew John, to create a mansion of sheer impressiveness are still clear. Feelings of sorrow mingle with awe at this impressiveness which is enhanced as one wanders around the grounds, with views over the gardens towards the chapel tower and the twin pillars above the chapel east windows.

The house did, however, evolve after the gardens in an endeavour to match the splendour of the grounds. It is difficult to commit to print a description that justifies their richness. Each turn brings a scene different to the last and one can only wonder at the vision Charles Talbot brought to fruition. Mature specimens of many varieties of tree and shrub can be found, set in a garden kept meticulously by the estate. Alton Towers boasts one of the largest gardens in the country and even when the car parks appear full, it is possible to find quiet corners, for the estate extends to some 600 acres.

The gardens gained effect through 'impressiveness of sheer profusion' as one writer put it. The practice of carpet bedding of flowers in parks originated here, but on a scale to fit the overall concept – far greater than is possible today. Scattered at strategic points can be found a 'Chinese' pagoda fountain, a corkscrew fountain, a Gothic temple, a splendid range of conservatories, bandstand, three-storey Stonehenge, etc. There is also a Swiss cottage built to house a blind Welsh harper who played at the earl's pleasure and from where a splendid view of the valley containing the garden can seen. Close to the boating lake end of the valley is the Choragic Monument with a bust of Charles Talbot with the fitting inscription 'He made the desert smile'. For today's visitors, the estate provides two large cafeterias, an amusement park, a huge model railway, scenic railway, cable car and gift shop. There is parking accommodation for 12,000 cars, 500 coaches, two hotels, and a well-laid out caravan site at the north-west end of the grounds. Sufficient, one might think to have impressed even Charles Talbot.

However, one suspects that most of today's visitors to Alton Towers are more interested in the state-of-the-art rides and the pleasure-giving village which has been created. Now with its own hotels on site, it is one of Europe's top pleasure parks.

ALTON TO ROCESTER

Alton is now a fashionable residential area but the old part of the village still keeps its charm. In the centre is the old village lock-up – a round stone-built building now with its door opened and with a 'body' inside! There are several public houses with good dining facilities. Above the village is the site of Bertram de Verdun's castle. Destroyed after the Civil War, remains of the curtain wall survive, including a tall tower, but all is on private land. The earl rebuilt it to Pugin's design and it is now a preparatory school. Verdun founded the church here and died in 1192 on the third Crusade under Richard I.

Old Village lock-up

Like most villages, Alton had a mill on the Churnet. Until 1734, it was a corn mill leased from the Shrewsburys. In that year the leaseholder, Robert Bill of Farley, entered into a partnership agreement with Thomas Patten and others and the mill was converted into a brass wire strip mill.

When the canal was built the mill pond was on its proposed course and lengthy arguments ensued before the canal was built across part of the mill pond – hence its elongated appearance today. The mill has been modified over the years but an inscription 'T P & Co 1736' still survives inside. The railway followed the line of the canal at Alton and although this has also gone now, the station has been retained, preserved by the Landmark Trust. The station was built to the design of Pugin in keeping with the Towers, and had first-class status, at the earl's insistence.

Patten did not renew the lease to the mill in 1828, and transferred operations to Oakamoor. It was subsequently used as a colour mill, but the occupier was bankrupt by July 1834. A cotton mill existed further downstream from the works, being established around 1787.

Above: Alton Railway Station. Below: Crumpwood weir

By 1817, it had been converted into a corn mill. A tanyard also existed at Alton in 1817, but was advertised for sale in 1832.

Alton was on the route of a medieval salt road from Cheshire to Ashbourne, Belper and Nottingham. The road originally crossed the Churnet at a ford, but by 1608 there was a bridge for the packhorse trains laden with their panniers of salt. Although still marked on nineteenth-century OS maps this bridge has long since gone, but Salters Bridge Lane remains. Alton has several good quality inns offering food and accommodation.

Below Alton, the valley begins to widen. Intriguing remains of the canal are noticeable, particularly at Crumpwood where the canal crossed the Churnet at river level. At Denstone, the valley has lost the beauty, which has characterised it from Cheddleton. The River Dove is not far away and both rivers unite just south of Rocester. Denstone is a small village, with little to interest the passing visitor. Nearby is Denstone College, a preparatory school, formerly the home of the Heywoods. A couple of miles to the west of the College is Croxden Abbey, and although in ruins it has far more to interest the visitor than its fellow Cistercian Abbey at Dieulacress, near Leek. The majority of the buildings date from the twelfth and thirteenth centuries and the west front, complete with its arch, survives. The site is, however, now crossed by a road and much of the church has

Croxden Abbey

disappeared, including the whole of the north and east sides. In spite of this there is still much to see and it is well worth a visit; it is situated off the Rocester to Tean road.

Rocester itself is also worth a visit, mills survive on the rivers Churnet and Dove, which flow to the west and east respectively of the village. The mill on the Dove was built by Sir Richard Arkwright in 1782. It is typical of the architecture of the period, a style that is reflected in other mills he built, such as the Masson Mills at Cromford. The most noteworthy item at Rocester is obviously the J. C. Bamford excavator manufacturing plant. From here JCB excavators are shipped all over the world. The factory has been carefully landscaped to merge into the rural environment and three large lakes surround the southern and eastern sides. Rocester now boasts a yachting centre and a 26-acre leisure park provided by the firm, together with a modern factory able to offer its employees both a high quality working environment and social facilities, and all from a business that started from nothing after World War II.

Although Alton is one of the most beautiful (and is certainly the most visited) parts of the Churnet Valley, the lower reaches are in contrast much less frequented. There is a certain amount of walking country, but the footpaths are mainly across agricultural land and lack the character of the higher tracts. In just over four miles the Churnet joins its sister stream, the Dove. Both of these river valleys are full of interest and natural beauty; every Staffordshire countrygoer has explored the Dove, but fewer know the Churnet. Hopefully, this guide will remedy that situation, for no one really knows Staffordshire who hasn't wandered the moorlands, woodlands and secret ways of the delectable Churnet Valley.

The Churnet is entirely a Staffordshire river, and the ridge-lands surrounding it also belong to this county. Those who take the trouble to explore the area covered in this little book will discover that Staffordshire is a Cinderella among counties, with rich rewards of a unique variety, for the discriminating visitor.

Blackbrook Zoological Park

Winkhill, Leek, Staffs (off A523 on road to Ellastone and Alton Towers) Large collection of birds, animals, reptiles and fish in 60 acres of land. Children's farm and pets corner; conservation and education programme. Gift shop and tea room.
Tel: 01538 308293
www.blackbrookzoologicalpark.co.uk

Foxfield Railway

Caverswall Road Station, Blythe Bridge, Stoke-on-Trent ST11 9EA. A 5½-mile journey on a former mineral line. Over 30 preserved steam and diesel locos. Tea room and shop.
Tel: 01782 396210/643507
www.foxfieldrailway.co.uk

CHEADLE

Situated to the west (or south!) of the valley is the town of Cheadle. A small market town, it is particularly well known for its splendid Roman Catholic Church (the one with the spire), built in the 1840s by Pugin. At a time when an excellent church could be built for under £10,000, this cost over £40,000. It is the best Victorian Tudor Gothic ecclesiastical building anywhere. Paid for by the Earl of Shrewsbury, it is a remarkable reminder of a far-sighted benefactor and his architect: like Leek, Cheadle is a good place to stay while exploring the area.

ACCOMMODATION

The Tourist Information Centres can direct you to a wide choice, but don't forget the farms and rural communities, that also offer splendid accommodation!

Fungi in Crowgutter Wood

Tourist Information Centres

ASHBOURNE:
13 Market Place, Ashbourne, Derbyshire DE6 1EU
Tel: 01335 343666. www.derbyshiresdales.gov.uk

Carparks: Shaw Croft – Main carpark in town centre.
   Free one at Cokayne Centre, off Cokayne Ave.
Toilets: Shaw Croft carpark, Bus Station, Recreation Ground
   and Union Street, off the Market Place.
Market Days: Thursday & Saturday.
Leisure Centre: Clifton Road. Tel: 01335 343712.

CHEADLE:
Cheadle Council Connect, 15a-17 High Street, Cheadle,
ST10 1AX. Tel: 01538 483860. www.staffordshire.gov.uk

Carparks: Tate Street, town centre.
Toilets: On Tate Street carpark.
Market Days: Tuesday, Friday and a small one on Saturday.
Leisure Centre: 01538 753331.

LEEK:
1 Market Place, Leek, Staffs ST13 5HH
Tel: 01538 483741. www.staffsmoorlands.gov.uk

Carparks: There are numerous carparks in the town centre.
Toilets: Market Street and Moorlands House (Council Office).
Market Days: Wednesday (outdoor), Wednesday, Friday
   & Saturday (indoor), Saturday (Flea market, outdoor).
Leisure Centre: Brough Park Leisure Centre 01538 373603.

Ashbourne Editions
Ashbourne Hall, Cokayne Ave, Ashbourne, Derbyshire, DE6 1EJ
Tel: 01335 347349 Fax: 01335 347303

1st edition

ISBN: 1-873775-196-1

© Lindsey Porter 2005

All rights reserved. No part of this publication may be reproduced, stored in a retrieval system or transmitted in any form or by any means, electronic, mechanical, photocopying, recording or otherwise without the prior permission of Ashbourne Editions.

Design & cartography: James Allsopp
Printed by: Gutenberg Press, Malta
Page 1: Consall Forge